DATE DUE

DEMCO 38-296

Chemicals
in Action

States of Matter

Chris Oxlade

Heinemann Library
Chicago, Illinois

Customer Service 888-454-2279

Visit our website at www.heinemannlibrary.com

Designed by Tinstar Design
Illustrations by Jeff Edwards
Originated by Ambassador Litho
Printed by Wing King Tong in Hong Kong

06 05 04 03
10 9 8 7 6 5 4 3

Library of Congress Cataloging-in-Publication Data
Oxlade, Chris.
    States of matter / Chris Oxlade.
       p. cm. -- (Chemicals in action)
    Includes bibliographical references and index.
    ISBN 1-58810-199-1
    1. Matter--Properties--Juvenile literature. [1. Matter.]   I.
  Title.
    QC 173.36 .O94 2001
    530.4--dc21
                        2001000104

Acknowledgments
The Publishers would like to thank the following for permission to reproduce photographs: pp. 4, 5, 9, 10, 11, 17, 19, 32, 36, 37, 38 Science Photo Library; pp. 7, 18, 20 Robert Harding; p. 12 Telegraph Colour Library; pp 13, 15, 21, 25, 31, 33, 35, 39 Trevor Clifford; p. 23 R. Maisonneure/Science Photo Library; p. 24 Tony Stone; p. 25 Mary Evans Picture Library; p. 27 Chris Bonington; p. 29 Ace Photos.

Cover photograph reproduced with permission of Bruce Coleman.

The publishers would like to thank Ted Dolter and Dr. Nigel Saunders for their assistance in the preparation of this book.

Some words are shown in bold, **like this.** You can find out what they mean by looking in the glossary.

Contents

Chemicals in Action 4

Three States of Matter 6

Solids 8

Density of Solids 10

Families of Solids 12

Crystals 14

Liquids .16

Properties of Liquids 18

Water 20

Gases 22

Gas Pressure 24

Air and the Atmosphere 26

Changes of State 28

More Changes of State 30

Energy for Changes 32

The Water Cycle 34

Mixtures 36

Other Ways to Separate 38

The Periodic Table 40

Common Elements 42

Common Chemicals 43

Glossary 44

Experiment Results 47

Further Reading 47

Index 48

Chemicals in Action

What's the link between rocket engines, medicine, gemstones, and icebergs? They are all solids, liquids, or gases—or they use solids, liquids, and gases to work. Solids, liquids, and gases are all states of matter. Our knowledge of these states of matter is used in making chemicals, in engineering, in medicine, and in many other areas of science.

The study of solids, liquids, and gases is part of the science of chemistry. Many people think of chemistry as something that scientists study by doing experiments in laboratories with special equipment This part of chemistry is very important. It is how scientists find out what substances are made of and how they make new materials—but this is only a tiny part of chemistry. Most chemistry happens far away from laboratories, in factories and **chemical plants.** It is used to manufacture an enormous range of items, such as synthetic fibers for fabrics, drugs to treat diseases, explosives for fireworks, **solvents** for paints, and fertilizers for growing crops.

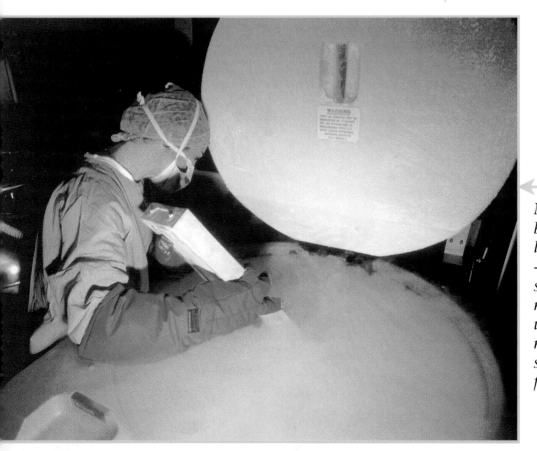

Nitrogen gas becomes a liquid below -196°C (-321°F), so liquid nitrogen is often used to keep medical specimens frozen.

*Solids often come in the form of beautiful crystals. These are crystals of the **element** sulfur.*

About the activities

There are several activities in the book for you to try. They will help you to understand some of the chemistry in the book. Some of the activities are demonstrations. Doing them will demonstrate a scientific concept. The other activities are experiments. An experiment is designed to help solve a scientific problem. Scientists use a logical approach to experiments so that they can conclude things from the results of the experiments. A scientist first develops a hypothesis, which might be the answer to the problem, then designs an experiment to test the hypothesis. He or she then observes the results of the experiment and concludes whether or not the results show the hypothesis to be correct. We know what we do about chemistry because scientists have carried out millions of experiments over hundreds of years. Experiments have helped us to understand why different substances are solids, liquids, and gases and why they have the **properties** they do.

Doing the activities

All the activities in this book have been designed for you to do at home with everyday substances and equipment. They can also be done in a school laboratory. Always follow the safety advice given with each activity, and ask an adult to help you when the instructions tell you to.

Three States of Matter

Most materials are solids, liquids, or gases. These are called the three states of matter. For example, wood is a solid, water is a liquid, and the air around us is made up of different gases.

Of the thousands of different substances we have on Earth, most are solids at everyday temperatures. Only a few are gases or liquids.

Properties of solids, liquids, and gases

A solid is a substance that keeps its shape. It does not flow like a liquid does or fill a space like a gas does. You can't easily **compress,** expand, or change the shape of most solids, because the **particles** in them are joined firmly together. There are some exceptions to this rule. For example, rubber is a solid, but it can stretch and bend without breaking. There are various families of solids, such as **metals** and plastics. And there are solids with regular shapes, called **crystals.** The **properties** of many solids make them useful materials for manufacturing items.

A liquid is a substance that flows. It has no definite shape like a solid does. It will flow to the lowest point that it can, so it always fills the bottom part of a container. Like solids, liquids are difficult to compress because their particles are closely packed together. Liquids such as oil are used in many machines.

A solid cannot flow, a liquid flows into the bottom of a container, and a gas flows to fill a container.

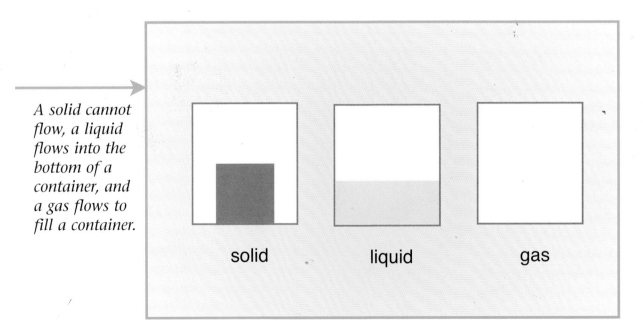

solid   liquid   gas

A gas is a substance that fills a space and flows to match the shape of the space it is in. Gases are easy to compress. Gases and liquids are both called **fluids** because they can flow.

There is a fourth state of matter, called plasma, that rarely exists naturally on Earth. Plasmas are commonly found in fluorescent lights.

Solid to liquid to gas

When we say that a substance is a solid, liquid, or gas, we usually mean in everyday conditions. This is, at the temperature inside a building, often called room temperature, and under normal **atmospheric pressure.** Many substances can exist in all three states of matter, depending on the conditions. The most common of these is water. Water can be a solid (ice), a liquid (water), or a gas (water vapor).

A change of state occurs when a substance changes from one state to another. For example, when ice melts, it is going through a change of state from a solid to a liquid. These changes are usually caused by a change in temperature —like ice melting when the temperature rises—but they can also be caused by a change in **pressure.**

Rock heated deep under Earth's surface melts into liquid rock called **magma.** *This flows out of volcanoes as lava.*

The atomic theory

Throughout this book, the properties of solids, liquids, and gases, and their changes of state, are explained using a **theory** called the atomic theory. This theory states that substances are made up of tiny particles that can join to each other. These particles are **atoms** or **molecules.**

Solids

Simply put, a solid is a substance that has a definite shape. This means that a solid object, such as this book, cannot change to become a completely different shape. It cannot flow like a liquid or a gas can. A solid also has a definite **volume.** It cannot be **compressed** into a much smaller space or stretched to fit into a much larger space. Most solids have high **densities,** which means that even small solid objects feel heavy.

Inside a solid

All substances, whether they are solids, liquids, or gases, are made up of tiny **particles** of matter far too small to see, even with a powerful microscope. These particles are either individual **atoms** or **molecules.** A molecule is a particle made up of two or more atoms connected to each other by links called chemical **bonds.**

In a solid, each particle is attached strongly to the particles around it by chemical bonds. The bonds are like tiny springs, with each end attached to a particle. The particles are fixed in their positions and cannot move. In **crystals,** the particles are arranged in regular rows and columns.

The particles in a solid are arranged in a regular pattern and are joined firmly to their neighboring particles by chemical bonds.

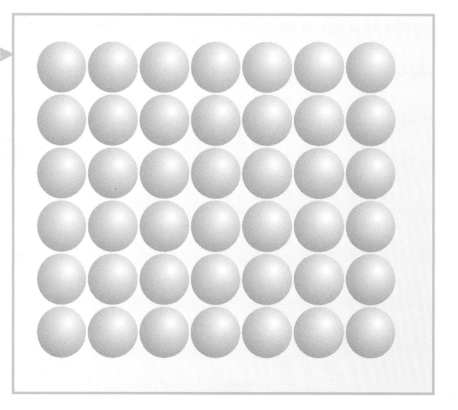

Compressing and stretching

Particles in a solid are packed tightly together and therefore cannot be easily compressed. However, most solids can be stretched a tiny bit. When they are stretched, the bonds are stretched a bit so the particles are pulled slightly further apart. The particles themselves do not change size, only the bonds do. The bonds are similar to springs, and when the force stretching them is removed, they return to their original shape—and so does the solid.

If the bonds between particles are stretched too much they break. When a very brittle solid, such as a china plate, is stretched, the bonds break suddenly and the china snaps. In **metals,** such as copper, the particles can move past each other without their bonds breaking, so they can be stretched into new shapes. Such solids are described as **malleable.**

In a few solids, such as rubber, the particles are huge, curly molecules containing thousands of atoms. These solids are easy to stretch and bend because the molecules can uncurl and straighten before they break.

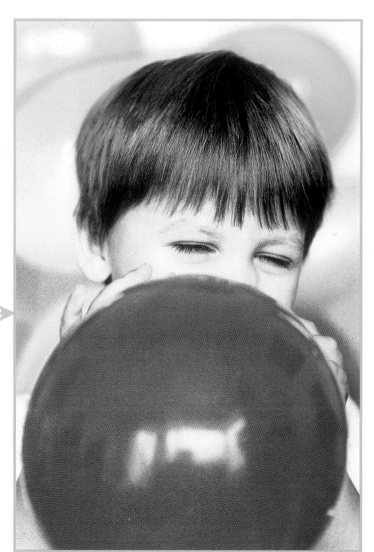

The rubber in a balloon can stretch to several times its natural size. If you stretch the rubber too far, however, the molecules will break and separate and the balloon will pop!

Density of Solids

Density is a measure of the heaviness of a substance. It is measured in pounds per cubic foot (lb/ft³) or grams per cubic centimeter (g/cm³). An object made of a substance that has a high density weighs more than an identical object made of a substance of lower density. The heavier the **particles** in a substance, and the more closely packed together, the more dense the substance is. Most solids, such as iron and marble, have high densities because the particles are packed closely together. Solids that have a low density, such as wood and some plastics, are not pure solids because they have air spaces inside.

Expansion and contraction

Although the particles in a solid cannot move from place to place, they can vibrate. The hotter a solid becomes, the more vigorously the particles vibrate.

As a solid is heated, its particles vibrate faster. The particles take up slightly more space, so the solid expands. Most solids don't expand much. For example, if a steel rail 330 feet (100 meters) long were heated so that its temperature rose by 100°C (212°F), it would only get 5 inches (12 centimeters) longer. As a solid cools, its particles vibrate more slowly and it **contracts.** You can think of the vibrating particles as people dancing in a packed room. The more energetically they dance, the more space they take up!

This is an expansion joint at the end of a road bridge. It has gaps that the bridge can expand into when the weather is hot.

Hard and soft solids

Some solids, such as **crystals** of bath salts, are quite soft and easy to scratch or break. Other solids, such as diamonds, are extremely hard and very difficult to scratch or break. Scientists use a scale of hardness to show how hard a solid is. H1 is the softest and H10 is the hardest. A **mineral** called talc has a hardness of H1, steel has a hardness of H5, and diamond has a hardness of H10.

The hardness of a solid depends on how its particles are arranged and the strength of its **bonds.** In soft solids, like talc, the particles are joined with weak bonds. In very hard solids, like diamonds, the particles are joined to all their neighbors with strong bonds.

Talc, a very soft mineral, has a hardness of H1.

Heat conduction

Heat energy travels through solids by a process called **conduction.** The heat is passed from one particle to the next. If you put a **metal** spoon in a hot drink, heat energy will spread up the spoon from particle to particle, gradually making the handle hot. Energy always passes from quickly vibrating, hotter particles to slowly vibrating, cooler particles—until both particles are vibrating at the same rate.

Families of Solids

We can group solids with similar **properties** into families, such as **metals,** ceramics, plastics, and stone. The properties of the solids in each family make the solids useful to us for different purposes.

Metals and alloys

About 75 percent of all **elements** are metals. Elements such as iron, copper, and aluminum are all metals. All metals are solids at room temperature, except mercury, which is a liquid. Metals are good **conductors** of heat and electricity. They are **malleable,** so a piece of metal can be hammered into different shapes without breaking. This would be impossible with an object made from a brittle material such as glass. Metals are also **ductile,** so a block of metal can be gradually drawn into a long, thin wire.

Metals are used to make a huge range of things, from bridges and cargo ships to tiny **electronic components.** Many of the metals we see every day in machines, furniture, and coins are **alloys.** An alloy is a **solution** of different metals or of a metal and a **nonmetal.** Making a metal into an alloy improves its properties for certain jobs. The most common alloy is steel, which is an alloy made up of iron with a small amount of carbon. Steel is stronger and more malleable than iron.

Most metals are very strong. This steel framework will hold up the walls and floors of a new building.

Plastics

Plastics are solids made from chemicals **extracted** from oil, gas, and plants. There is a wide range of plastics, each one suitable for a different job. For example, plastics used in casings for machines such as computers are rigid and hard, but plastics used for shopping bags are flexible and soft. Plastics can be made resistant to heat, which means they do not burn or go soft when heated, and resistant to chemicals, which means they do not react with chemicals such as **acids.** They are also easy to shape by molding.

Ceramics

Ceramics are materials such as pottery, china, and glass. They are made from substances found in the ground, such as rock, clay, and sand. For example, pottery is made by heating wet clay in a kiln, which makes the clay harden. Ceramics are very good insulators against heat and electricity and are resistant to chemicals. For example, strong acids are stored in glass bottles, because glass does not react with acids.

Experiment: Good and bad conductors

PROBLEM: Which materials are good conductors of electricity and which are bad conductors?

HYPOTHESIS: If you put pieces of material into a simple circuit containing a battery and bulb, the bulb will light only if the material is a conductor.

EQUIPMENT
flashlight
aluminum foil
tape
objects to test, made of metal, wood, plastic, ceramic, etc.

Experiment steps

1. Cut a strip of aluminum foil about half an inch (1 centimeter) wide. If you want to test large objects, make your strip a long one.

2. Dismantle the flashlight. Use tape to stick one end of the foil strip to the bottom of the battery. Wrap the other end of the foil around the side or the metal base of the bulb (do not let it touch the bottom of the bulb).

3. To test an object to see if it conducts electricity, touch the object with the top of the battery and the bottom of the bulb at the same time.

RESULTS: Which materials make the bulb light up? Which materials do not? What does this tell you about their ability to conduct electricity? You can check your results on page 47.

Crystals

Some solids come in the form of **crystals.** The **particles** in a crystal are arranged neatly in a regular pattern called a **crystal lattice,** with each particle attached to its neighbors. Solids that come in the form of crystals are described as crystalline. Examples of everyday crystal substances are sodium chloride (table salt) and granulated sugar.

Because of the neat arrangement of their particles, many crystals have straight edges and flat faces. Different crystalline substances form crystals that have different numbers of faces and edges at different angles to each other. For example, sodium chloride forms cubic crystals with six faces, like tiny dice.

Forming crystals

The formation of crystals is called **crystallization.** Crystals form in two ways. They form when a molten substance cools down to become a solid. Or they form when a **solution** containing a substance cools or evaporates and the substance separates from the solution. During crystallization, particles join together to make a solid crystal. If this happens slowly, large crystals are formed. If it happens quickly, smaller crystals are formed. For example, igneous rocks, formed when **magma** cools slowly underground, have large crystals. But when magma cools quickly above ground, the rocks formed have small crystals.

Shown here are two simple crystal shapes and how the particles are arranged inside them. The shape of each crystal matches the arrangement of the particles in it.

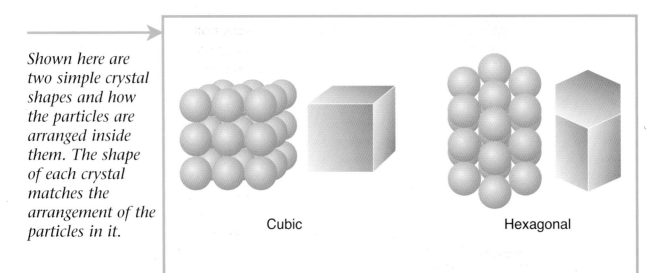

Cubic

Hexagonal

Experiment: Growing crystals

PROBLEM: How can you make crystals?

HYPOTHESIS: Crystals are often left when a liquid cools down or dries up. Cooling a solution of a substance might make crystals grow.

> **EQUIPMENT**
> alum powder
> glass jars
> cotton thread
> popsicle stick

Experiment steps

1. Fill a glass jar with warm (not boiling) water. Add a teaspoon of alum powder and stir the water to help the powder **dissolve.** Keep adding powder and stirring until no more powder will dissolve. This is called a saturated solution.

2. Allow the leftover powder to settle at the bottom of the jar. Pour the solution into another jar, leaving the powder behind.

3. Tie a short piece of cotton thread to a popsicle stick and hang it in the solution. (You might need to put a weight on the end of the thread to keep it inside the solution.) Leave the jar where it will not be disturbed.

RESULTS: Wait a few days and check the jar from time to time. What happens to the thread? Why do you think this is happening? You can check your results on page 47.

Liquids

A liquid is a substance that flows to fill the bottom of the container that holds it. A liquid does not have a definite shape like a solid does, but it does have a definite **volume.** This means it cannot easily be **compressed** into a much smaller space or stretched into a much larger space. At room temperature, only a few **elements** and **compounds** are liquids. The most common is water. Most other liquids, such as fruit juices, are **solutions** made up mostly of water.

Inside a liquid

The **particles** in a liquid are attracted to each other, but they do not form permanent chemical **bonds** with each other. They are closely packed together, but they are always on the move. They are like people packed in a room who move around in little groups but occasionally change from one group to another.

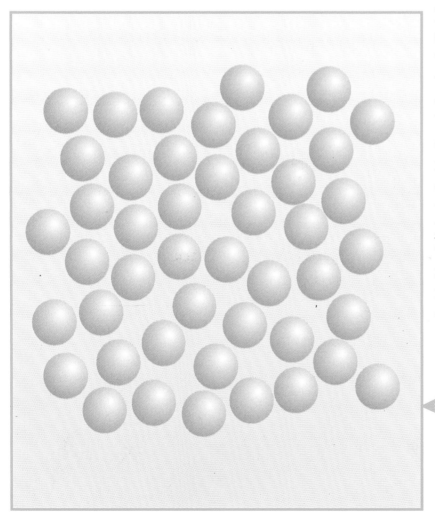

Most liquids have slightly lower **densities** than solids, because their particles are not so closely packed together. Water has a density of 62.4 pounds per cubic foot (1 gram per cubic centimeter). Mercury is the only metal that is a liquid at room temperature. Its density is 850 pounds per cubic foot (13.6 grams per cubic centimeter).

The particles in a liquid are closely packed and randomly arranged. They can move around each other.

Compressing and stretching

A liquid can change shape easily. However, it cannot easily be compressed into a smaller space because its particles are packed closely together. So you cannot compress a plastic bottle full of water. But a liquid can be compressed a tiny bit more than a solid. When a liquid is compressed, the particles are squeezed closer together. If the compressing force is removed, the liquid returns to its original volume. If you try to stretch a liquid, its particles soon break apart, so the liquid breaks up into droplets. That's why a thin stream of water from a faucet breaks into droplets.

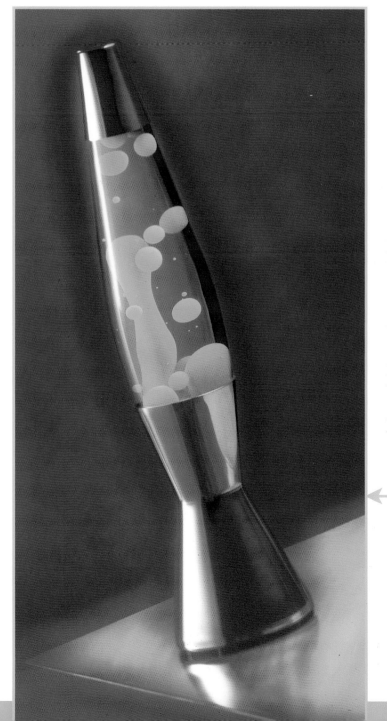

Expansion and contraction of liquids

Inside a liquid, the particles are constantly moving around. The hotter the liquid, the faster the particles move. If a liquid is heated to a higher temperature, its particles move faster than before. This makes them collide with each other more often, and so they take up more space. In turn, this makes the liquid expand slightly. When the liquid cools, it goes back to its original volume.

Liquid at the bottom of a lava lamp is warmed, expands, and rises to the top. At the top of the lamp, the liquid cools, contracts, and sinks back to the bottom of the lamp.

Properties of Liquids

How easily a liquid flows is called its viscosity. Some liquids, such as water, have low viscosity and flow easily out of a jar if it is tipped over. Other liquids, such as cooking oil or molasses, have high viscosity and flow slowly out of a container. Liquids made up of long **molecules,** such as oil, are very viscous because the molecules tangle with each other.

Convection currents

Liquids are not good **conductors** of heat. However, heat can travel through a liquid by a process called **convection.** If one part of a liquid is heated, it expands slightly, floats upward, and is replaced by cooler liquid, which in turn is heated. The currents created in the liquids are called **convection currents.**

Diffusion in liquids

Liquids can mix naturally with each other in a process called **diffusion.** For example, if you put a drop of food coloring in some water, the color eventually spreads completely through the water. This happens because the **particles** in a liquid are always on the move. Diffusion happens slowly because the particles keep colliding with each other.

Liquid pressure

A liquid will press on any object that is in it. This pressing is called liquid **pressure.** The pressure increases deeper down into the liquid. Submarines need very strong hulls to prevent being crushed by the water pressure when they are in very deep seas.

The arm of this hydraulic backhoe is moved by liquid that is pumped into the arms through pipes.

Blaise Pascal (1623–1662)

French mathematician and physicist Blaise Pascal studied pressure in liquids and gases. He was the first person to realize that liquids press on objects in all directions, not just downward. This is known as Pascal's principle. He went on to invent the hydraulic press and the first mechanical calculating machine.

Experiment: Convection currents

PROBLEM: How can you see convection currents?

HYPOTHESIS: By adding some colored dye to water and heating the water, the convection currents may be visible.

EQUIPMENT
large glass jar
dish
food coloring

Experiment steps

1. Fill the glass jar with cold water. Stand the jar in a dish and leave it for ten minutes so that movements in the water settle down.

2. Pour some hot water into the dish. Carefully put several drops of food coloring into the water in the jar.

RESULTS: Watch what happens to the color. Why do you think this is happening? You can check your results on page 47.

Water

Water is a tasteless, colorless liquid. It is the most common liquid on Earth and is necessary for animals and plants to live. It is also the only substance that we regularly see in all its three states: ice, liquid water, and water **vapor.** The **particles** that make up water are **molecules,** each containing two hydrogen **atoms** and one oxygen atom. The chemical formula for water is H_2O.

Ice

Ice is the solid form of water. Most substances become more dense when they turn from liquid to solid, but ice is unusual because it is less **dense** than liquid water. This is why ice floats on the top of water. On a frozen lake, the layer of ice acts as a blanket, keeping the water underneath from freezing too. Under the ice, life goes on as normal for fish and other aquatic animals.

Water vapor

The gaseous form of water is called water vapor. There is always some water vapor in the air, but you cannot see it. You can only tell that it is there because when it hits a cold surface, such as a window, it cools and turns into small droplets of liquid water. The word *steam* is sometimes used instead of *water vapor,* and it is also used to describe the clouds that come out of a hot kettle or pan. Steam is actually made up of water droplets that form as the water vapor leaves the kettle spout and cools to become a liquid again.

Ice is only slightly less dense than water, so most of this iceberg is hidden under the water.

Water is a poor conductor

1. This tube contains water, some steel wool pushed into the bottom, and an ice cube on top. The steel wool reduces the **convection currents** going up and down the tube, but still allows heat to travel through the water by **conduction.**

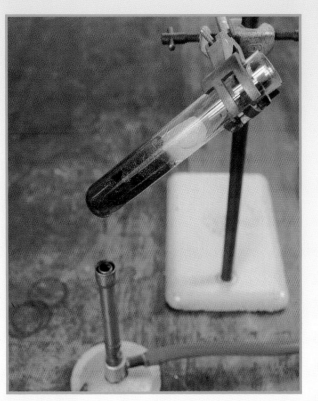

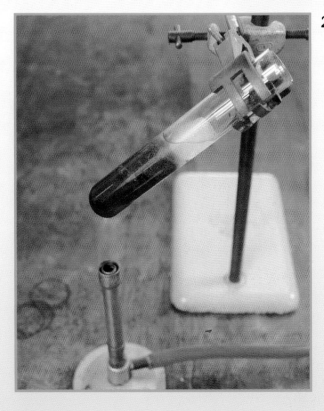

2. When the end of the tube is heated and the water boils, the ice does not melt. This is because the heat does not travel through the water. Water is a poor **conductor** of heat.

Gases

A gas is a substance that expands to fill the container it is in. A gas does not have a definite shape, which means that it can flow and change shape like a liquid can. It also does not have a definite **volume,** which means that it can be compressed into a much smaller space. It expands when it is allowed to.

Inside a gas

The **particles** in a gas are **atoms** or **molecules.** They travel at high speed, bouncing off anything they hit—including each other. They are not attached to each other in any way. You can think of the particles as being similar to people running about in a room, bouncing off the walls and each other! You could make the room smaller or bigger, and the people, the "gas," would still fill it.

Gases have **densities** thousands of times lower than solids and liquids because of the spaces between their particles. The density of a gas increases if the gas is squeezed into a smaller volume and decreases if it expands to fill a larger volume.

The particles in a gas are widely spaced and randomly arranged. They can move about at high speed in any direction, often crashing into each other.

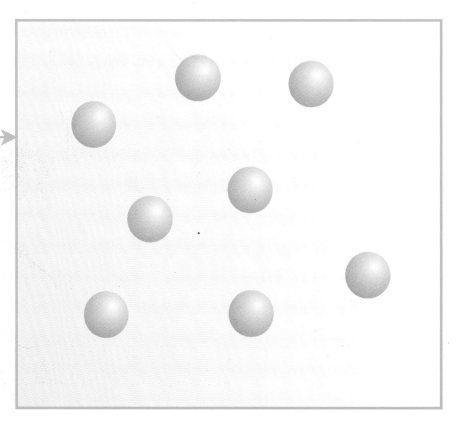

Common gases

The most common gases on Earth are found in the air that makes up Earth's **atmosphere.** They include nitrogen and oxygen. Other gases, such as hydrogen and ammonia, are used for the production of chemicals, such as fertilizers. They are produced in **chemical plants.** Natural gas, used for cooking and heating, is a **fossil fuel** made up mostly of methane.

Diffusion in gases

Like liquids, gases can also spread and mix with each other by **diffusion.** You can smell food because the gases given off by the food diffuse through the air to your nose. Diffusion is faster in gases than it is in liquids because the particles in a gas are traveling so fast. However, it is still a relatively slow process because the particles in the gas constantly hit each other and change direction.

Plasma

There is another state of matter, called plasma. It only exists naturally at extremely high temperatures or very low pressures. It is formed when the **electrons** in the atoms that make up a gas become separated from their **nuclei**. Plasma has different **properties** than a gas. For example, a plasma is a good **conductor** of electricity. On Earth, air is changed to plasma during a lightning strike, and there is plasma inside a working fluorescent lamp.

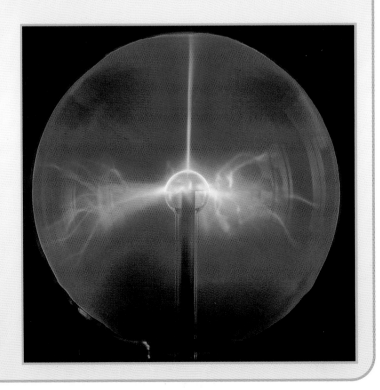

Gas Pressure

The **particles** of a gas bounce off any object they hit. In fact, millions of gas particles bounce off of you every second. They also bounce off the sides of any container the gas is in. These collisions create a push on the surface of objects, called gas **pressure.** The more frequent the collisions and the faster the particles move, the higher the gas pressure.

Increasing gas pressure

Changing the temperature or **volume** of a gas changes its pressure. Imagine a container full of gas. If the gas is heated, its particles move faster. This causes them to hit the sides of the container harder and more often, so the gas pressure increases. Now imagine a syringe full of gas. If the plunger is pushed in to decrease the volume of the gas, the particles in the gas have a smaller space in which to move. They hit the sides of the container more often, increasing the gas pressure.

Gases and heat

Gases are poor conductors of heat. Energy cannot be passed from one particle to the next because the particles are not closely packed. This is why gases are used in insulating materials. For example, a down comforter traps pockets of air that stop the heat escaping from your body. Heat can move through a gas by **convection,** as it does through liquids.

Pressurized air makes this jackhammer work. Machines that use gas to work are called pneumatic machines.

Jacques Charles (1746–1823)

Frenchman Jacques Charles was a government official, teacher and physicist. He is famous for his experiments with gases. In 1787, he discovered that gases expand at the same rate when they are heated. This is the basis for Charles' Law, which states that the volume of a gas is proportional to its temperature. Charles also made the first flight in a hydrogen-filled balloon, in 1783.

PROF. CHARLES.

HYDROGEN-GAS BALLOON.

Experiment: Expansion and contraction of air

PROBLEM: What happens to the volume of air when it is heated and cooled?

HYPOTHESIS: Trapping some air in a balloon, then changing the temperature while measuring the size of the balloon, will show if the air changes in volume.

EQUIPMENT
balloon
tape
freezer

Experiment steps

1. Blow up the balloon to a size that will just fit into your freezer. Carefully stick a length of tape around the outside of the balloon.

2. Put the balloon in the freezer for a few minutes and then look at the tape. What has happened to the air in the balloon?

3. Remove the balloon from the freezer so that it warms up again.

RESULTS: Watch again what happens to the tape. Do you think the temperature is responsible for these changes? Why? You can check your results on page 47.

Air and the Atmosphere

What we call "air" is actually a blanket of gas called the **atmosphere** that surrounds Earth. Air is made up of several different gases. It is colorless, tasteless, and odorless. The gases in air are necessary for life and take part in chemical reactions such as burning.

Gases of the air

All but a tiny fraction of the air is made up of nitrogen (78 percent) and oxygen (21 percent). The remaining one percent is mainly argon, from the group of gases called the noble gases.

Animals and plants need oxygen, which they take from the air, for **respiration.** There is normally some water **vapor** in the air as well. On very humid days, water vapor can make up more than four percent of the air. This water vapor comes from water on Earth's surface that **evaporates** in the Sun. It plays an important part in the water cycle, because it allows water to be transported through the atmosphere.

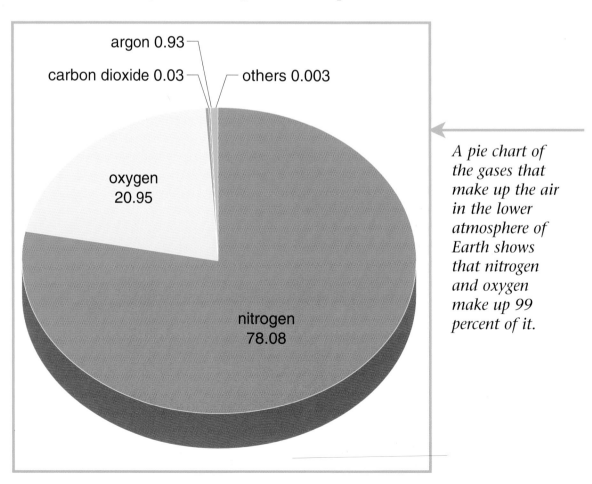

argon 0.93

carbon dioxide 0.03

others 0.003

oxygen
20.95

nitrogen
78.08

A pie chart of the gases that make up the air in the lower atmosphere of Earth shows that nitrogen and oxygen make up 99 percent of it.

The air gets thinner as you move up through the atmosphere. Mountaineers often need extra oxygen to breathe at high altitudes, so they carry oxygen in tanks.

Carbon dioxide makes up just 0.03 percent of the air, but is needed by plants for **photosynthesis.** It is also the main greenhouse gas. Greenhouse gases trap heat from the Sun in the atmosphere, similar to the way glass traps heat inside a greenhouse. Without this greenhouse effect, Earth would be a freezing, lifeless planet.

However, increasing amounts of carbon dioxide in the atmosphere, created by the burning of **fossil fuels,** are making the atmosphere warmer. This enhanced greenhouse effect is causing **global warming.** The air also contains other polluting gases such as sulfur dioxide, which causes **acid** rain.

The ozone layer

Ozone is a gas that is a form of oxygen. Each **molecule** of ozone contains three oxygen **atoms** instead of two, as in normal oxygen molecules. Its formula is O_3. The ozone layer is 6 to 30 miles (10 to 50 kilometers) above Earth's surface. The high concentration of ozone there reduces the amount of harmful rays from the Sun that can reach Earth's surface.

Changes of State

A change of state occurs when a substance changes from one state of matter to another. For example, when ice changes to liquid water, the water is said to have changed states. Changes of state usually occur when the temperature of a substance changes. As the temperature increases, substances change from solid to liquid and then from liquid to gas. As the temperature decreases, they change from gas to liquid and then from liquid to solid. A substance always goes through changes of state at the same temperature. For example, pure water always changes from ice to liquid water at 0°C (32°F). It always turns from liquid to gas at 100°C (212°F).

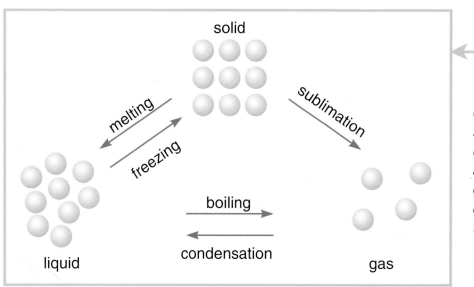

This diagram shows the triangle of changes of state from solid to liquid to gas and back again. Sublimation is the change of state from a solid straight back to a gas.

Physical and reversible changes

Changes of state are physical changes. This means that when a substance changes state, only its physical **properties** change. Its chemical make-up stays the same. Changes of state are also reversible changes. This means that if a substance changes state, it can change back again. For example, if a solid piece of metal is heated until it melts, it will always turn back to a solid when it cools again.

Not all substances can exist in different states. For example, if wood is heated it never melts. Instead, when wood gets hot enough, it burns. Burning wood is an example of a chemical change. It creates a new substance. It is also a permanent change, because the wood cannot be brought back once it burns.

Melting and freezing

Melting is the change of state from solid to liquid. The temperature at which this change occurs is called a substance's melting point. The melting point of ice is 0°C (32°F). The melting point of iron is 1,535°C (2,795°F). Freezing is the change of state from liquid to solid. The freezing point of a substance is the temperature at which the liquid becomes solid. The freezing point is equal to the melting point.

Boiling and condensation

Boiling is the change of state from liquid to gas. It is the opposite of **condensing.** A substance's boiling point is the temperature at which it changes from liquid to gas. The boiling point of water is 100°C (212°F). The boiling point of iron is 2,861°C (5,182°F).

Condensation is the change of state from gas to liquid. The temperature at which a gas condenses is called its dew point.

Winter ice in rivers and lakes turns back to water when temperatures rise above 0°C (32°F).

More Changes of State

Changes of state occur when the **particles** in solids, liquids, and gases either break away from each other or join together. Here's what happens during each change of state.

When a solid is heated, its particles vibrate more and more. When it reaches a certain temperature—its melting point—some of the **bonds** between the particles begin to break. This allows the particles to break free from their positions and begin to move around. When this happens, the solid has melted to become a liquid. If a liquid cools, its particles slow down. Eventually the bonds will form again, and the liquid will become a solid again.

When a liquid is heated, its particles move around faster and faster. When it reaches a certain temperature—its boiling point—the particles break free from each other completely. The liquid has boiled to become a gas. If a gas cools, its particles slow down. Eventually bonds will begin to form again, and the gas will **condense** to become a liquid.

*Water **vapor** has cooled and condensed to form droplets of liquid water on this window. We often call these droplets condensation.*

Evaporation

Evaporation is also a change of state from liquid to gas, but it can happen even if the temperature of a liquid stays below its boiling point. In a liquid, particles moving near the surface sometimes escape from the surface, forming a gas above the liquid. This process is called evaporation. Puddles gradually dry up because of evaporation. They do not boil away.

Changing volumes

Most substances increase in **volume** slightly when they melt, because the particles in a liquid are slightly further apart than they are in a solid. Water is an exception to this rule, because ice is slightly less **dense** than water. All substances increase greatly in volume when they boil, because particles in a gas are widely spread.

What state?

You can predict what state a substance will be in at a certain temperature by looking at a table of melting and boiling points. For example, the metal mercury has a melting point of -39°C (-38°F) and a boiling point of 357°C (675°F), so at room temperature—about 20°C (68°F)—it is a liquid. In extremely cold weather, mercury would be a solid. In a very hot oven, it would change into a gas.

Changing melting and boiling points

If conditions stay the same, the melting and boiling points of a substance stay the same, too. The melting and boiling point change if the substance is not pure or if the air **pressure** around it changes. For example, the melting point of salt water is a few degrees below 0°C (32°F). On high mountains, where the air pressure is lower, the boiling point of water is several degrees below 100°C (212°F).

Mixtures like *chocolate tend to soften and melt gradually rather than melt at an exact temperature.*

Energy for Changes

We know that a substance has to be heated to raise its temperature to its melting or boiling point. Once it has reached its melting or boiling point, increasing the temperature does not make the substance hotter, it makes it change state instead. The increased temperature provides the energy needed to break the **bonds** between the **particles.**

Even metals melt, given enough heat.

For example, water heated in a kettle gets hotter until its temperature reaches its boiling point of 100°C (212°F). Then the water boils to make water **vapor.** Its temperature stays at 100°C (212°F) because the energy from the heating element is used to turn the water to water vapor.

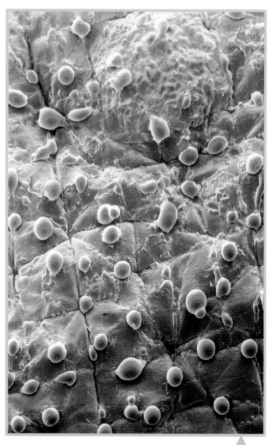

Cooling down

Changes of state are used to cool things down. For example, putting ice in a drink cools the drink because the energy needed to melt the ice comes from the drink. In a similar way, sweating when it is hot cools you because heat energy from your skin is used up when the sweat **evaporates** from your skin.

Beads of sweat on skin gradually evaporate, using up heat energy in your skin.

Experiment: Temperature changes

PROBLEM: What happens to the temperature of a substance as it changes state?

HYPOTHESIS: Heating a substance gently will add heat to it at a constant rate. Measuring its temperature will show what happens as the substance gets hotter and changes state.

EQUIPMENT
saucepan
wooden spoon
cooking thermometer, with range between 0°C (32°F) and more than 100°C (212°F)
clock or watch

Experiment steps

1. Wrap some ice cubes in an old dish towel. Crush the ice cubes by standing on them or ask an adult to hit them gently with a hammer. Put the ice in a pan, add a small amount of cold water, and stir. Use the thermometer to measure the temperature of the mixture. Record the temperature.

2. Ask an adult to put the pan on the stove, heat it gently, and stir with a wooden spoon. Measure and record the temperature every minute. Make a note of the time when all the ice has melted.

3. When the water has been boiling for 1 minute, turn the heat off. Do not let the pan boil dry.

4. Draw a graph with time along the horizontal axis and temperature along the vertical axis. Plot the temperature for each minute.

RESULTS: What do you notice about the temperature before the ice melts? After the ice melts, does the temperature change? Why do you think this happens? You can check your results on page 47.

The Water Cycle

Towering dark clouds, pouring rain, and fast-flowing rivers are all evidence of Earth's water on the move. The water circulates between the oceans and seas, the **atmosphere,** the land, and the rivers. This circulation is called the water cycle. It happens as water changes from liquid water to water **vapor** and back again. It also occurs as water vapor is carried along in the atmosphere. If these changes of state did not occur, water would never get onto land, so animals and plants could not live there.

Water in the air

Water is constantly **evaporating** from the world's oceans, seas, lakes, and land into the air above. Moving air carries the water vapor away. As this damp air rises higher in the atmosphere, it cools. This causes some of the water vapor to change back to liquid water, which forms tiny droplets we see as clouds. If the droplets get big enough, they fall to the ground as rain or snow, which soaks into the ground or runs off into streams and rivers. The water eventually returns to the sea.

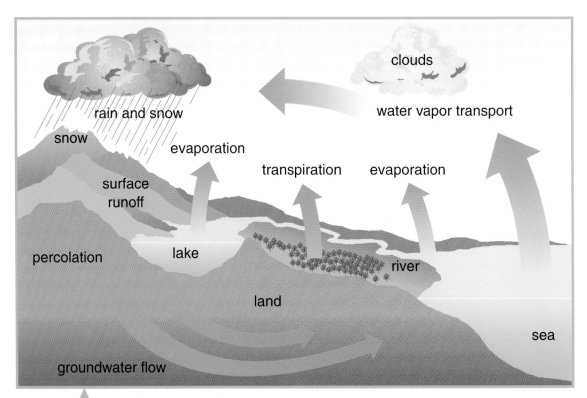

In the water cycle, water evaporates from the seas and land into the air, condenses to form clouds, falls as rain and snow, and then soaks into the ground or runs back into the sea by way of rivers.

Demonstration: A water cycle model

Here you can see how to make a simple model of the water cycle. It will help you to understand how water circulates around the world.

Demonstration steps

1. Place the dish on one end of the box. Cut a strip of cardboard in a rectangular shape and fold it down the middle to make a "V" shape (printed side up). This is your river channel. Tape the channel to the other end of the box so that any water flowing down the channel will drip into the dish.

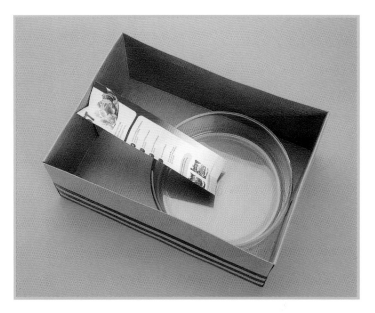

2. Pour some hot water into the dish. Cover the box with clear plastic food wrap. Put some ice on the wrap above the cardboard channel.

3. Watch what happens under the ice and on the channel. Water should evaporate from the dish (a model of the sea), and the water vapor will spread through the box. When it hits the cold wrap under the ice it **condenses** (forming model clouds). The rainwater then drips onto the channel and runs back into the dish.

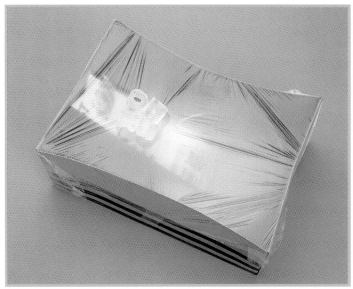

Mixtures

A **mixture** is a substance that contains different **elements** and **compounds** that are not joined together by chemical **bonds.** Some mixtures contain just solids, just liquids, or just gases. However, others are mixtures of substances in two or three different states. Some mixtures are **solutions,** formed when one substance (the **solute) dissolves** in another—the **solvent.**

Separating mixtures

Chemists often need to separate mixtures into their different parts. For example, they might need to **extract** a useful chemical from a mixture, remove the impurities from a substance to purify it, or figure out what substances are in a mixture.

To separate mixtures, chemists make use of the fact that the different elements and compounds in the mixture have different **properties,** such as different boiling points or **densities.** Four of the main ways of separating mixtures are filtration, **evaporation,** distillation, and chromatography.

These building panels contain solid foam, a mixture containing plastic and gas.

Evaporation

Evaporation is a method for separating a dissolved solid from a solution. For example, you could use evaporation to extract the salt from salt water. The salty solution is put into a wide container so that a large area of solution is in contact with the air. The solvent (the water) gradually evaporates, in the same way that a puddle dries up and is lost into the air. The **particles** of the solid (the salt) do not evaporate, so eventually only the solid is left in the container.

Distillation

Distillation is a method of separating a solvent from a solution. For example, you would use distillation if you wanted to retrieve the water from salt water. The solution is put in a flask and heated until the solvent boils to make a gas. The gas flows along a tube into a separate container, where it cools and **condenses** back into liquid. The solute is then left in the flask.

Fractional distillation is used to separate a mixture of liquids that have different boiling points. The mixture is put in a flask and gradually heated. Each liquid in the mixture boils at a different temperature to make a gas, and the different gases are collected and condensed to turn them back into liquids.

Fractional distillation is used at this chemical plant to separate the mixture of compounds in crude oil.

Other Ways to Separate

Filtration is used to separate a **mixture** of a liquid and a solid that has not **dissolved.** The mixture is poured through filter paper, which has very tiny holes in it. The liquid can get through the holes but the solids cannot. For example, if you filter muddy water, the water **molecules** pass through the holes in the paper but the larger **particles** of soil are trapped. The clean water can then be collected in a container.

Chromatography

Chromatography is used to figure out the different parts of a mixture. Scientists use it to test whether substances are pure or to find whether two mixtures contain the same parts. The simplest type of chromatography is paper chromatography. A blob of a mixture, such as an ink (which is a mixture of dyes), is put on a piece of filter paper. The end of the paper is then placed in a **solvent,** such as water, that dissolves the mixture. The solvent moves through the paper, carrying the dissolved dyes with it. Different dyes are carried different distances before they are left on the paper.

Water is the most common solvent, but it is not the only one. Other solvents, such as trichloroethane, are used to dissolve substances that don't dissolve in water. For example, acetone is used to dissolve nail varnish, trichloroethane dissolves grease, and turpentine dissolves glossy paint.

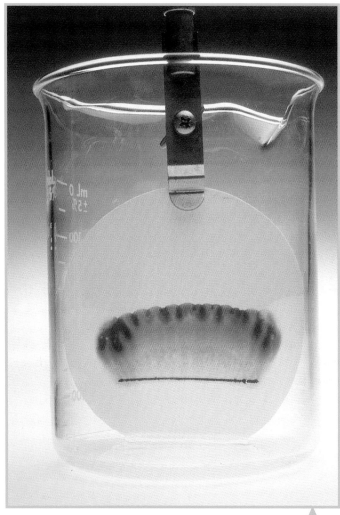

Paper chromatography is used to separate the different chemicals in a sample of ink.

Experiment: Filtering muddy water

PROBLEM: How can you clean muddy water?

HYPOTHESIS: Mud is made up of tiny particles of rock, so pouring muddy water through filter paper should remove these particles.

Experiment steps

1. Fill a glass jar halfway with water and stir in some soil. The soil particles will not dissolve. They will stay solid, making a mixture.

2. Put a coffee filter inside the strainer over the bowl. If you do not have one, you can use paper towels.

3. Pour the muddy water slowly into the strainer. Allow time for the water to drain through.

RESULTS: Carefully unfold the coffee filter. What do you see? Why do you think this has happened? You can check your results on page 47.

The Periodic Table

The periodic table is a chart of all the known **elements.** The elements are arranged in order of their atomic numbers, but in rows, so that elements with similar **properties** are underneath each other. The periodic table gets its name from the fact that properties repeat themselves every few elements, or periodically. The position of an element in the periodic table gives an idea of what its properties are likely to be.

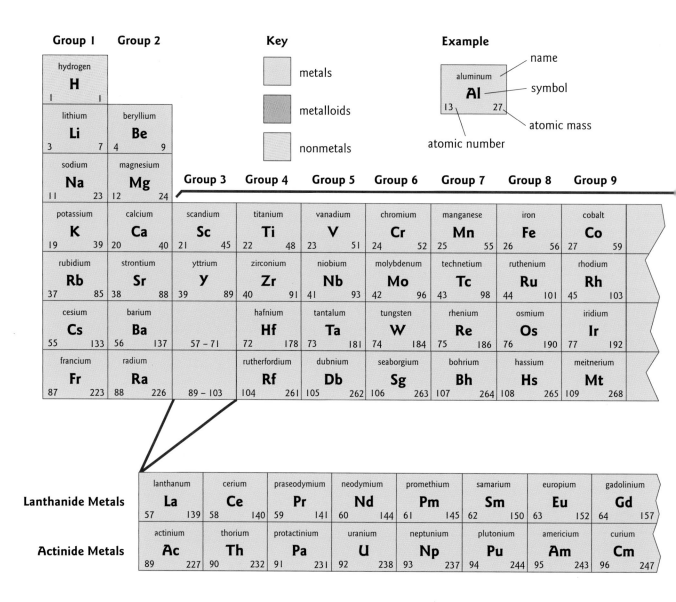

Key
- metals
- metalloids
- nonmetals

Example

aluminum — name
Al — symbol
13   27 — atomic mass
atomic number

Group 1	Group 2
hydrogen **H** 1 1	
lithium **Li** 3 7	beryllium **Be** 4 9
sodium **Na** 11 23	magnesium **Mg** 12 24

Group 3	Group 4	Group 5	Group 6	Group 7	Group 8	Group 9
potassium **K** 19 39 calcium **Ca** 20 40						

Group 1	Group 2	Group 3	Group 4	Group 5	Group 6	Group 7	Group 8	Group 9
potassium **K** 19 39	calcium **Ca** 20 40	scandium **Sc** 21 45	titanium **Ti** 22 48	vanadium **V** 23 51	chromium **Cr** 24 52	manganese **Mn** 25 55	iron **Fe** 26 56	cobalt **Co** 27 59
rubidium **Rb** 37 85	strontium **Sr** 38 88	yttrium **Y** 39 89	zirconium **Zr** 40 91	niobium **Nb** 41 93	molybdenum **Mo** 42 96	technetium **Tc** 43 98	ruthenium **Ru** 44 101	rhodium **Rh** 45 103
cesium **Cs** 55 133	barium **Ba** 56 137	57 – 71	hafnium **Hf** 72 178	tantalum **Ta** 73 181	tungsten **W** 74 184	rhenium **Re** 75 186	osmium **Os** 76 190	iridium **Ir** 77 192
francium **Fr** 87 223	radium **Ra** 88 226	89 – 103	rutherfordium **Rf** 104 261	dubnium **Db** 105 262	seaborgium **Sg** 106 263	bohrium **Bh** 107 264	hassium **Hs** 108 265	meitnerium **Mt** 109 268

Lanthanide Metals

lanthanum **La** 57 139	cerium **Ce** 58 140	praseodymium **Pr** 59 141	neodymium **Nd** 60 144	promethium **Pm** 61 145	samarium **Sm** 62 150	europium **Eu** 63 152	gadolinium **Gd** 64 157

Actinide Metals

actinium **Ac** 89 227	thorium **Th** 90 232	protactinium **Pa** 91 231	uranium **U** 92 238	neptunium **Np** 93 237	plutonium **Pu** 94 244	americium **Am** 95 243	curium **Cm** 96 247

Groups and periods

The vertical columns of elements are called groups. The horizontal rows of elements are called periods. Some groups have special names:

Group 1: Alkali **metals**
Group 2: Alkaline earth metals
Groups 3–12: Transition metals
Group 17: Halogens
Group 18: Noble gases

The table is divided into two main sections: the metals and **nonmetals.** Between the two are elements that have some properties of metals and some of nonmetals. They are called semimetals or metalloids.

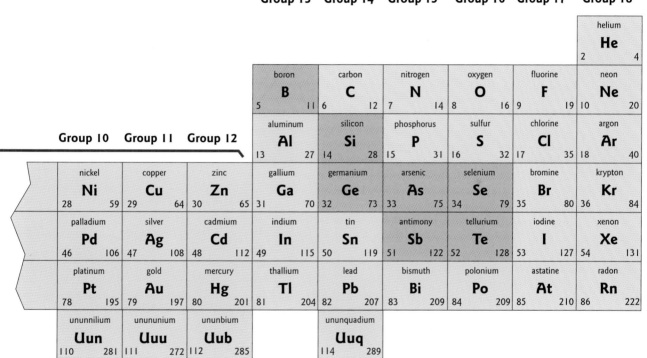

Common Elements

Here is a table of the most common **elements** from the periodic table that you may come across at home or in the laboratory. The table lists whether the element is a solid, liquid, or gas at room temperature and its melting and boiling points. (Melting and boiling points are for pure chemicals).

Element	Symbol	State at room temperature	Melting point (°C)	(°F)	Boiling point (°C)	(°F)
hydrogen	H	gas	-259	-434	-253	-423
helium	He	gas	-272	-458	-269	-452
lithium	Li	solid	180	356	1,342	2,448
carbon	C	solid	3,730	6,746	4,830	8,726
nitrogen	N	gas	-210	-346	-196	-321
oxygen	O	gas	-218	-360	-183	-297
fluorine	F	gas	-220	-364	-188	-306
neon	Ne	gas	-249	-416	-246	-411
sodium	Na	solid	98	208	883	1621
magnesium	Mg	solid	650	1,202	1,090	1,994
aluminum	Al	solid	660	1,220	2,519	4,566
silicon	Si	solid	1,414	2,577	2,900	5,252
phosphorus	P	solid	44	111	280	536
sulfur	S	solid	113	235	444	831
chlorine	Cl	gas	-101	-150	-34	-30
argon	Ar	gas	-189	-308	-186	-303
potassium	K	solid	63	145	759	1,398
calcium	Ca	solid	842	1548	1,487	2,709
iron	Fe	solid	1,535	2,795	2,861	5,182
copper	Cu	solid	1,083	1,981	2,595	4,703
zinc	Zn	solid	420	788	907	1,665
bromine	Br	liquid	-7	19	59	138
silver	Ag	solid	961	1,762	2,210	4,010
tin	Sn	solid	232	450	2,270	4,118
iodine	I	solid	114	237	184	363
gold	Au	solid	1,063	1,945	2,970	5,378
mercury	Hg	liquid	-39	-38	357	675
lead	Pb	solid	327	621	1,744	3,171

Common Chemicals

Here is a table of some common chemicals that you may come across at home or in a laboratory. The middle column shows their formulas.

Chemical	Symbol	Components
Gases		
hydrogen	H_2	hydrogen
oxygen	O_2	oxygen
chlorine	Cl_2	chlorine
nitrogen	N_2	nitrogen
carbon dioxide	CO_2	carbon, oxygen
nitrogen dioxide	NO_2	nitrogen, oxygen
Liquids and solutions		
water	H_2O	hydrogen, oxygen
hydrochloric acid	HCl	hydrogen, chlorine
sulfuric acid	H_2SO_4	hydrogen, sulfur, oxygen
nitric acid	HNO_3	hydrogen, nitrogen, oxygen
sodium hydroxide	$NaOH$	sodium, oxygen, hydrogen
Solids		
sodium chloride	$NaCl$	sodium, chlorine
magnesium oxide	MgO	magnesium, oxygen
calcium carbonate	$CaCO_3$	calcium, carbon, oxygen
copper sulfate	$CuSO_4$	copper, sulfur, oxygen

Glossary

acid liquid that is sour to taste, can eat away metals, and is neutralized by alkalis and bases. Acids have a pH below 7.

alloy solution of a metal combined with a nonmetal or another metal. Alloys are often stronger than pure metals.

atmosphere layer of air that surrounds Earth

atmospheric pressure force that the air in the atmosphere applies to all the objects in it

atom extremely tiny particle of matter. An atom is the smallest particle of an element that can exist and that has the properties of that element. All substances are made up of atoms.

bond chemical connection between two atoms or molecules

chemical plant place where chemicals are manufactured

compound substance that contains two or more different elements joined together by chemical bonds

compress to squeeze into a smaller shape or space

condense to change from a gas to a liquid

conduction when electricity or heat passes through a substance called a conductor

conductor substance through which electricity or heat passes

convection when heat moves from place to place in moving gas or liquid

convection current movement that carries heat through a gas or liquid when one part of the gas or liquid is heated

crystal piece of a substance that has flat sides and straight edges

crystal lattice regular arrangement of particles inside a crystal

crystallization process that forms crystals

density amount of a substance (or mass) in a certain volume. Density is measured in grams per cubic centimeter or pounds per cubic foot.

diffusion movement of particles through a liquid or gas caused by the random movement of the particles

dissolve when the particles of a solid mix with those of a liquid so they seem to disappear into the liquid

ductile capable of being drawn out into a thin strand

electron extremely tiny particle that moves around the nucleus of an atom

electronic component device such as a capacitor or transistor in an electronic circuit

element substance that contains just one type of atom. An element cannot be changed into simpler substances.

evaporate to change state from liquid to gas at a temperature below the normal boiling point

extract to remove a substance from a mixture of substances

fluid substance that flows, such as a liquid or a gas

fossil fuel fuel formed from the remains of ancient plants and animals. Coal, oil, and gas are fossil fuels.

global warming gradual warming of Earth's atmosphere, probably caused by the burning of fossil fuels

magma molten rock under Earth's crust

metal any element in the periodic table that is shiny and conducts electricity and heat well. Most metals are also hard.

mineral any chemical that occurs naturally in the rocks of the earth's crust

mixture substance made up of two or more elements or compounds that are not joined together by chemical bonds

molecule type of particle made up of two or more atoms joined together by chemical bonds. The atoms can be of the same element or different elements.

nonmetal any element in the periodic table that is not a metal. Most nonmetals are gases.

nucleus central part of an atom, made up of protons and neutrons. The plural form is **nuclei.**

particle very tiny piece of a substance, such as a single atom or molecule

photosynthesis chemical reaction in green plants that makes food. In photosynthesis, carbon dioxide and water react together using energy from sunlight to make sugar and oxygen.

pressure force pushing on a certain area

property characteristic of a substance, such as its strength, melting point, or density

respiration chemical reaction that happens in all living cells. In respiration, sugar reacts with oxygen to produce carbon dioxide and water. Energy is released for our cells to use.

solute substance that dissolves in a solvent to make a solution

solution substance made when a solid, gas, or liquid dissolves in a liquid, solid, or gas.

solvent solid, liquid, or gas that a substance dissolves in to make a solution

theory ideas about how something works

vapor the gas form of a substance that exists below the substance's boiling point

volume space that something takes up

Experiment Results

page 13: Any metal object, such as a key, that you test should make the light bulb glow. Something like a pencil, which is not a metal, will not. This shows that metals are good conductors of electricity and that other materials are not.

page 15: After a few days, an alum crystal should form on the thread. It forms because there is more alum in the solution than the water could hold.

page 19: The color moves up and down the jar, showing that warm water flows up the jar and is replaced by cool water from above.

page 25: The tape wrinkles when the balloon is cooled. This shows that air contracts when it is cooled, and it expands again when it heats up.

page 33: At the start of the experiment, the temperature should stay at 0°C (32°F), because all the heat goes into melting the ice. Once the ice has melted, the heat is used to increase the temperature of the liquid. At the end, all the heat goes into boiling the water to make water vapor.

page 39: When you unfold the coffee filter it should be full of soil. The coffee filter has allowed the water molecules to pass through, but not the solid soil particles. This has separated the soil and the water.

Further Reading

Fleisher, Paul. *Liquids and Gases: Principles of Fluid Mechanics.* Minneapolis: Lerner Publishing Group, 2001.

Fullick, Ann. *Chemicals in Action.* Chicago: Heinemann Library, 1999.

Gardner, Robert. *Science Project Ideas about Kitchen Chemistry.* Berkeley Heights, N.J.: Enslow Publishers, Inc., 2002.

Moje, Steven W. Cool Chemistry: *Great Experiments with Simple Stuff.* Madison, Wisc.: Turtleback Books, 2001.

Oxlade, Chris. *Illustrated Dictionary of Chemistry.* Tulsa, Okla.: EDC Publishing, 2000.

Stwertka, Albert, and Eve Stwertka. *A Guide to the Elements.* New York: Oxford University Press, 1999.

Index

air 23, 26-27, 36
atmosphere 23, 26-27
atmospheric pressure 7
atomic theory 7
atoms 7, 8, 20, 22

boiling/boiling points 29, 30, 31, 32, 36, 43

ceramics 13
changes of state 7, 28–35
    experiments 33, 35
    physical and reversible changes 28
Charles, Jacques 25
chemical bonds 8, 9, 11, 16, 30, 36
chromatography 36, 38
compounds 16, 36
condensation 20, 29, 30, 37
conduction 11, 12, 13, 18, 21, 23, 24
convection 18, 19, 24
cooling down 10, 14, 32
crystals 6, 8, 11, 14–15

densities 8, 10, 16, 20, 22, 36
diffusion 18, 23
distillation 36, 37

elements 16, 36, 40–41, 42, 43
evaporation 26, 30, 34, 36, 37
expansion and contraction 10, 17, 25
experiments 5, 13, 15, 19, 21, 25, 33, 35, 39
    safety 5

filtration 36, 38, 39
fluids 7
fractional distillation 37
freezing/freezing points 29

gas pressure 24-25
gases 4, 6, 7, 22–27, 30, 36
    common gases 23
    convection 24
    definition 22
    densities 22
    diffusion 23
    experiment 25
    greenhouse gases 27
    noble gases 26
    properties 7
    volume 22, 24, 25
global warming 27

heat energy 11, 12, 21, 24, 32

ice 7, 20, 28, 29, 31, 32, 33

liquid pressure 18, 19
liquids 4, 6, 7, 16–21, 30, 36, 38
    convection 18, 19
    definition 16
    densities 16, 20
    diffusion 18
    expansion and contraction 17
    experiments 19, 21
    properties 6
    viscosity 18
    volume 16

malleability 9, 12
melting/melting points 29, 30, 31, 32, 43
metals and alloys 6, 9, 11, 12, 41-42
mixtures 16, 26, 36–39
    separating 36
molecules 7, 8, 18, 20, 22, 27, 38

ozone layer 27

particles 6, 7, 8, 9, 10, 11, 14, 16, 17, 18, 20, 22, 23, 24, 30, 31, 32, 37, 38
Pascal, Blaise 19
periodic table 40, 41, 42
plasma 7, 23
plastics 6, 10, 12

solids 4, 6, 7, 8–15, 30, 36, 38
    definition 8
    densities 8, 10-11
    expansion and contraction 10
    experiments 13, 15
    families 12–13
    hard and soft solids 11
    malleable solids 9, 12
    properties 6
    volume 8
solutions 36, 37

temperature changes 7, 10, 28, 33

viscosity 18
volume 8, 16, 22, 24, 25, 31

water 7, 16, 18, 20–21, 28, 31, 32, 34, 37, 38, 39
water cycle 26, 34, 35
water vapor 7, 20, 26, 32, 33, 34